Work Explained to Career Starters

How to end your job hunting with good decisions

Andreas A Landman

Copyright © 2018 Andreas Landman
All rights reserved.
ISBN-13: 9781730739699

Foreword

When I left university and started working in July 2003, I was in for a cultural shock. Being used to a largely like-minded group of people at school and university did not prepare me for the variety of the work environment.

The principles I received from my parents, however, did far more to prepare me. I knew who I was and whose I was and could stand my ground.

Many young adults enter the job market every year. Bright-eyed and bushy-tailed is the expression.

A first job can be daunting, and this book will help make it easier to treasure the opportunity given to a young adult entering the job market. After completing the job-hunting phase, the young adult must now make important decisions.

For

   Adolph and Hanlie Landman - my supportive, guiding and loving parents.

   Edith Landman - my supportive, caring, correcting and loving wife.

   Anika Lee and Aileen - my lovely daughters.

John 10:10

The thief comes only to steal and kill and destroy; I have come that they may have life, and have it to the full.

Jesus

Acknowledgements

A quick thank you to my dad, Adolph Landman, for giving me the idea to write this book and spending the time to read earlier versions of the book.

Jennifer Rault-Smith edited the book with great finesse.

My mentors remained true to themselves and me and made valuable comments

    Alexander Whaley

    Richard Garlick

    Philip Viljoen

    Johann van der Merwe

    Isabel Ferreira

Some mentees also made insightful comments

    Sibusiso Mnisi

    Yeshan Govender

Table of Contents

Welcome to work 1

   The Mission of the Company 2
   Structure of Companies 3
   Your Role 6

Different Backgrounds 9

   Household 10
   Income 11
   Heroes 12
   Education 13
   Exposure 17
   Background Summary 21

Getting the Job 23

   CV 24
   Interview 26
   Medical 27
   Summary of Getting the Job 28

Evaluate the Job 29

   Can you do this? 29
   Do you want to do this? 31
   Are you willing to live with the Salary Package? 32
   Summary of Job Evaluation 42

Keeping the Job 43

   Timekeeping 44
   On the Job Training 47
   Attitude 52
   Summary of Keeping the Job 62

Your Rights 63
Constitution 64
OHS Act 67
BCEA 68
Labour Relations Act 69
Compensation for Injury on Duty 70
Skills Development 71
EE 71
Summary of Rights 72
Last Sage Advice 73
Look After your Finances 73
Budget 74
Don't make babies 76
Lose the Booze 76
Summary of this Book 79

Welcome to work

Welcome to this book. Welcome to the work environment. Welcome to what is generally considered adulthood.

Welcome to "Work Explained to Career Starters."

Job hunting and then keeping a job is not easy - regardless of the country in which you live. This book will give you some insights into what is involved. This book is not a full description of work. This book puts the work environment in perspective, a perspective that might be unfamiliar to you.

You might have studied, or you might not have had the opportunity to earn a qualification after high school, but you are entering the work environment. You will feel as though you start from the bottom because you are starting from the bottom. You must get to know the people. You must find out where the toilets are. You must find out how to do things and how not to do things.

You are eager to earn a wage/salary - this is called making a living. Beware, you might change the emphasis of the sentence to be a desperate plea - "Is this what they call making a living." This book will not prevent such a plea. This book opens your eyes to some of the issues with being a beginner at work and you might end up saying - "I did the best I could with the opportunity the company gave me." I hope that you also add: "I have grown, and I am ready for the next step."

Let us dive into what work is, and the decisions you need to make.

The Mission of the Company

A company is usually established to make money by bringing people together in an organisational structure to achieve the goal of making money.

All companies have stakeholders.

"Stakeholders" is a term used to describe people or other companies that have an interest in the company.

In general, the biggest stakeholder is the shareholder. A shareholder is a person or persons who give money to the company so that the company can exist and operate. In return for this money (investment) the shareholder(s) want their money back, hopefully, more money than their initial investment in the company.

There is a common misconception that the shareholder(s) is the terrible fat cat making a lot of money on the back of the work of others. Why is the aforementioned a misconception? Because eventually, you will be a shareholder. The moment you have a retirement fund, you are a shareholder in some company or another. Your pension fund will invest your hard-earned money in companies. You also want to retire (when you are old and grey) with more money than you initially put into your retirement fund.

Other important stakeholders are the suppliers and customers of the company. The company is often dependent on the suppliers to supply them with the correct material to be able to have the workers work to fulfil the needs of the customers - with added value (or perception of value) so that the company can make money.

You are also a stakeholder. The employee. Often you might feel overlooked, but this does not mean that the company can overlook you. You can make or break the company. Hence there is a structure needed to protect you and protect the company.

Companies usually have a mission statement, which includes the purpose of the company, a picture of the future that describes what the company is working towards and the values used to make decisions.

The mission of the company is important to you as well. You might want to put some money in your pocket as soon as possible, but you will not be able to do so for long if you cannot work with the company - more about that later.

The company exists for a purpose. You either help the company in this purpose, or you don't. The company will exist with you or without you. I hope that you find a company where you can earn money, be fulfilled and contribute to the company so that the company is better because of you and you are better because of the company.

Many people distinguish between small and large companies. In law and as far as you are concerned there is very little difference. You are there to work and must comply with instructions.

Structure of Companies

A company consists of functional building blocks - meaning different types of work being done by teams who work together to achieve the mission of the company. You will find yourself in one of these functions. In modern companies, the lines between these functions are blurred, but we will not discuss that in this book. We will focus on a traditional view so that you know who is, who in the zoo.

There is a hierarchy. Hierarchy means you have a manager who has a superior who has a superior for several layers. The number of layers depends on the complexity of the company and often on the size of the company. The hierarchy means that one person looks out for others and give them instructions. There are other ways of describing this relation, but we will not go there.

Your first point of contact will often be the Human Resources function. They have several different roles. Amongst others they look at recruitment, hence your first point of contact. They make sure that there are job descriptions and job evaluations, and the accompanying advertisements and interview sheets to find you. The recruitment also involves making sure that your qualifications are not fake, you are who you say you are and that you do not have a background that is not acceptable to the company - some companies do not employ people with a criminal record, which might include drunk driving! Once you have been found, interviewed and accepted, Human Resources will make sure you have the necessary paperwork to join the company. Be warned; there is a lot of paperwork in the first couple of days of joining a company - practice your signature.

Another aspect of Human Resources is industrial relations, which deals with how you interact with the company. Making sure that when things are not as initially intended, you or the company changes their ways.

The payroll function pays you. The payroll function only pays you what your manager told them to pay you, so when in doubt first talk to your manager.

All functions stand, and fall based on the systems used to support their activities - this is mostly done on computers. The IT (Information and Technology) department can make or break the company quickly. Remember so can you.

The training function usually takes you by the hand or ear and inducts you into the ways of the company. This function will also look after your training needs in the future.

The safety, health, quality and risk functions in companies vary significantly - be aware of these. Forgetting any of these functions will cost you dearly.

The accounting department is there to look after the money the company has - to have money to pay you, the suppliers and get money from the customers. They report how much money the shareholder(s) are making. They evaluate the monetary effect of business decisions.

Procurement buys what the company needs to buy.

"Stores" makes sure that what the suppliers deliver is received, stored and issued as required.

Engineering makes sure that the machines are safe and in working conditions. Improvements and maintaining the buildings are also part of their job.

Operations or manufacturing makes sure that what the company procured is transformed into what the customers want.

Planning makes sure that the customer gets what they want when they want it.

"Sales" makes sure that the company knows what the customer wants and gets the customer to buy what he/she wants from the company.

Logistics makes sure the customer gets the products where they want it.

The technical function has several roles in product development and product manufacturing.

Industrial Engineering leads the charge in the improvement of the different functions.

Wow, what a lot of functions. You will have a job somewhere in one or many of these functions.

Your Role

"The circle of life..."

Yes, the one moment you are on top and the next moment you are at the bottom.

You achieve the status of being the big boy/girl in school, to land in the tertiary institution where you are led to believe you know nothing and have everything to learn. Then you end up on the street without a job. Job hunting. Some are not fortunate enough to have the tertiary institution as a step.

Regardless, you end up looking for a job. What will your role be? Often your role does not matter. You would be happy with an end to the endless job hunting. Remember, you will start at the bottom. You do not know where the toilets are unless you ask, are told or happen to see where they are.

Your initial role is to be a part in the function which is a part of the company. Your role is to make contributions (some small, some big) to the success of the company. You contribute by doing what you are told to do in the way you were trained to do the tasks. Following commands – both written and verbal – is what you do at work.

Eventually, you will be able to make and should be invited

to make improvement suggestions - how can the company do things better.

Remember, as the company improves, you improve.

You survived the first chapter. Good, now you know what companies are.

Let us see where and how you can fit in. How you can get into the job and then stay there.

Different Backgrounds

We are the sum of our experiences. We are the sum of our choices.

We are made by what happens to us and more so by how we choose to react to what happens to us.

Or so the sayings go.

The fact is, we are all different - even twins - who have the same DNA, but not the same fingerprints.

Don't worry we will not go into psychological or biological or biochemical differences in this book. We will focus on our background and how that influences who we are.

These differences determine what we know about work and how we handle work and the pressures of work. These differences determine how we handle authority and being told what to do. Face it, in the job environment you will be told what to do and how to do it. If you do not do what you are supposed to do in the way you are supposed to do it, you will land in trouble. The kind of trouble that might help you find the gate of the company permanently. Your manager also needs to do what he is told to do and do it correctly. Scary isn't. This is your everyone's lot in life.

Regardless of your background, you can be sure of one thing; you are in for a surprise. This book aims to minimise that surprise and make sure you have your job for as long as you are happy at the company you have chosen. Remember you might have the opportunity to have more than one position/career within the same company.

Now for some more philosophy. Often two necessary and sufficient conditions are required to create problems. Many young adults land in trouble because the general impression of young adults is that they are both entitled and crave immediate gratification. Feeling entitled and craving immediate gratification is not necessarily bad in and of itself. Just know that humbleness and patience will serve you well in the long run.

For your first job, the chances are that you are not special. I do, however, harbour the hope that if you are special, you do not allow anyone to put out the positive fire in you and that you allow yourself all opportunities to grow and maybe even become CEO (Chief Executive Officer or President) of a company someday.

So am I merely dreaming - not that dreaming is bad. NO! In a recent study[1], one of the best CEO's, Don Slager, started as a garbage truck driver.

Household

The household environment is not the same as the work environment, and no household is the same.

At home, you might have a mother, father and siblings.

You might be the responsible sibling, which means your job is important for the financial well-being of the family, not just for you at a personal level.

---

[1] https://capx.co/the-surprising-truth-about-what-makes-a-great-ceo/, downloaded November 1, 2018

You have an authority figure at home and at school. You are used to going to someone who takes charge of the situation - mother, father, uncle, aunt, grandfather, grandmother, teachers, principal and others. At work, the hierarchy is different, as discussed earlier.

The nature of your household will influence how you deal with the work environment. You might be dependent on others to look after you - in which case you will have difficulty at work. You might be used to ruling the roost - in which case you will have clashes at work.

Know that at work, the employer has responsibilities towards you and you have responsibilities towards the employer. Make sure you understand this and do your part.

Income

Having money is a privilege.

Not having money leads to wanting money.

Getting money does not necessarily lead to more money, nor happiness.

How you see money will influence how you see work.

Work is a means to an end, for most beginners. You work to get money to get a roof of some kind over your head and food in your stomach. Subsistence living is not easy but is the reality for most people.

If you have not handled your own money before, you might not be ready to handle the company's money.

Often you will be exposed to equipment at work, which costs at least nearly as much as you would earn in a decade of working. Therefore, handle with care. Let me say that again, handle all equipment as if you would need to replace it out of your pocket when it breaks. Hence, you will inevitably follow the safe operating procedures and do as the managers tell you.

Do not think you are better or worse than anyone else because of your historical income - no one likes someone with a chip on their shoulder. Do not be jealous or high and mighty. You will need to prove yourself first; then you should still be humble.

Work is a privilege, look after your work. Protect your job and those of your fellow employees.

Heroes

Describing what a hero is, is difficult. In my view, celebrities are often seen as heroes, even though they are often "merely" famous. Don't get me wrong, some celebrities use fame and sometimes their fortune to do amazing acts that enrich other people's lives.

To me, the heroes, are the unsung heroes. The father/mother who gets up at 04:00 to take three trips on different means of public transport to be at work by 05:45 only eating the first meal of the day at 10:00, if then. The ones who go to work day in and day out working with their hands and heart. Often these individuals are the backbone of the companies they work for, the backbone of their country. Unsung indeed, but heroes nonetheless.

Heroes come in different forms. In my experience with young adults starting jobs in South Africa, the hero is often the single mother cleaning someone else's home. And these heroes are to be honoured. My view is that the only way to honour their efforts is to emulate their spirit and work hard.

Think about your heroes. Think about what makes them heroes. Will you meet someone with those qualities in your job? Do you need to exhibit those qualities in your job? Do so.

Many young South Africans have grown up to know Nelson Mandela as the nation's hero. The fact that Nelson Mandela is a hero is true, and no one should be allowed to take away from what he has done. Know that many others also deserve to be remembered, if not hero-worshipped.

Education

I place a high value on education. You might not. You may place a high value on brawn.

We are all different.

Regardless of your view of education, you need to have the ability to follow instructions. These instructions are usually in written form; therefore, you need to be able to read and understand and to a large extent remember what you read. Learn.

The challenge is that at most levels of education, low levels of performance are deemed to be acceptable. Please note that at work this is not acceptable. For example, at school 30 % is the pass rate, at university 50 % is the pass rate and at work, 90 % is the pass rate. A big difference in mindset! At work, if you do not know what you are doing the equipment, you and the company are in danger. Therefore, the company can only let you work where they know you will be able to do things safely in line with the company way.

At a later stage of your career other levels of thinking - problem-solving and creative thinking - will be of value. At all stages of your work career, you are expected to tow the company line – follow management's instructions.

Regardless of your level of education, you can always learn. You would be surprised who can teach you. I have many times learned something from workers with no education past high school - why? Because the workers work with the equipment every day, they know best. The communication channel must go both ways and must always stay open.

School

As mentioned earlier you might not place a high value on your schooling. Please know that it is important to make sure you are successful at school - successful not regarding the school's standards, but regarding your standards.

Maybe you want to be the hot property at school - so be it. The future is far away.

The schooling systems in many countries do not

deliver workers to companies at the required level. Therefore, the standards of companies move to account for this lower standard at school. So, you might have made it through high school, but not in a way that is acceptable to the company. The company would, for example, only employ a worker with a 50 % mark in all subjects - therefore, making sure that you can read, write and learn at the requisite level.

If you do not have a high school record showing 50 % marks, you might want to take a year and focus on improving your marks - without the social pressures of being the big shot in school. Improving your high school marks might be worth more than going to a tertiary institution. Should you decide to go to a tertiary institution, you would have a better record and stand a better chance of getting admission and scholarship to the tertiary institution.

Never be ashamed of your schooling background. You might have attended a non-academic school, but at the end of the day, you got your high school pass. Now you must sell yourself.

Tertiary Education

Making sense of tertiary qualifications is beyond me. N, M, Degree, Diploma and so on?

Anyway, it does not make a difference now. You either have the qualification, or you do not have the qualification.

The question is whether you have the qualification required for the job for which you are applying. The qualification puts your foot in the door. You must push the door open and get inside and stay inside.

Make sure you give the full transcript to the potential employer and be ready to be interrogated.

Please do not give up on yourself. If you qualify, apply for the job.

If you do not qualify, write a cracker of a cover letter. Explain why, despite your qualification being in a different field or at a different level, you feel you are the best person for the job. You might have a passion for the work in the job, a passion that you no longer have for the field you studied in but have the necessary knowledge to contribute to the success of the company. Maybe you get a career change before your career even started.

Think of reality-shows some of us enjoy watching. We applaud those who stop their current job and follow their passion for singing or cooking. These applauses should be found for other career changes as well.

Part Time Jobs

Not everyone has had the opportunity to work before they apply for a job at a large company, but when you have had that opportunity, milk that opportunity. Any work experience and this includes working for non-profit companies, must be used to get the company to see that you have potential.

The consensus is that having worked for a year will ensure that you will find a job - this is why learnership and internship opportunities abound. Not having worked for a year, will make it significantly more difficult to get work opportunities.

The contents of this book is equally applicable to you

finding an opportunity as a learner or intern, so please read further and apply the data in this book to get something on your CV for the next work opportunity.

Exposure

Work and home will expose you to different environments and situations.

A simple example would be our general view of what is safe. At home, we regularly use a chair to get something off the top of a cupboard. At work, this would be an unsafe act and an unsafe condition - more on this later.

Another example is that lighting a fire to keep warm is completely normal (this is not a social comment). At work, you would not be able to light a fire to keep warm, at best you would be able to ask for a heater at some form of a meeting at some time in the future.

Some employees wake up in the morning to a warm shower (or bath if that is your thing) having gone to the loo without having to fear that the neighbours might see them. Others wake up in the dark have a cold basin wash and walk to refill the household water container.

Do not look at the differences between yourself and others. You may dream. You must aspire but be happy with what you have. Having the ability to earn a living - money to buy food - is something to make you proud. Be proud.

Your household background gives you an exposure level. If you have almost nothing, your circumstances have exposed you to nearly nothing. Not being exposed to a lot means that your work environment will expose you to new things - please keep this in mind when you communicate with your employer. Ask questions. Do not be afraid. If fear rules, speak to the human resources department. You must have the ability to discuss your exposure or lack thereof with your managers.

I remember a time when I found a squeegee mop in the waste bin. At that stage, I was angry until I looked at myself and realised that I did not take the responsibility to teach the employees how the mop works. I did not make it clear that the mop has a permanent and a replacement part. The understanding of the difference comes from the level of exposure - not intelligence.

Know that your manager needs you to get the job done, so help him/her to help you perform to the benefit of the company.

Exposure to Books

The saying goes: "Knowledge is Power", which is only partially true in the information age in which we live. We have access to significantly more data than our predecessors had.

More accurately, the application of knowledge is power.

I love reading books.

I remember an interview with a potential candidate who said he loved books, but when asked which book he is currently reading he said he does not have opportunities to get hold of books at this stage because he does not have money. I chased him out of the interview. Work requires resilience. Companies cannot have people sitting around who cannot help themselves.

What I said then, I will write here. Libraries are mostly free - except for the initial registration, which comes with a library card. You can read the newspaper in the library. You can also read the newspaper at some restaurants - go in buy a hot or cold drink and read the newspaper. If you must, go to different restaurants if they see that you only want to read the newspaper.

Most people have access to the world's knowledge in the palm of their hand - use the smartphone, some good free resources are as follows:

Gutenberg

Blinkist

News24.

At times you can find good free books on Kindle - maybe you found this book.

Of course, to be able to use a smartphone you need mobile data. Again, make use of free data provided by restaurants, malls and even the municipality.

Exposure to Technology

You hardly find any equipment that is not linked to a PC anymore. Use your smartphone to teach you how to interface with technology. Do not be afraid of technology.

Again, some libraries give you access to computers - make

use of these opportunities. See if you can enrol for courses that teach you the basics of word processing and using spreadsheets, which can be done on your phone as well.

Limited exposure to technology is not a large barrier to getting your first job but can be beneficial to get that job. Remember you are competing with others, who could be your friends, to get the scarce job. You are in a battle for survival.

Do not use the phone just as a phone. Not just as a gaming console. Learn how to set up the phone, how to read e-mail - get a free e-mail account and learn, learn, learn. Be careful not to be caught by phishing expeditions. Learn about tech security.

Exposure to Risk

Many, if not all, work environments are inherently more dangerous than staying at home.

Work might expose you to new dangers. Moving equipment, electricity, working at heights, and dealing with dust. Some of the material you might be handling is dangerous as well.

Your past exposure to risk will help you understand the new risks at work. Your past exposure to risk will help you ask questions to help you be safer at work.

Do not think because you have made it to some arbitrary age; you will double your age. Being safe is not a guarantee. You need to be aware of your surroundings. You can hone the skill of being aware of your surroundings no matter what your past exposure levels were. Walk around with open eyes. Do not look at the phone or drown out the sounds around you with earphones. Listen, look, be safe. Be that way at home, and you will be that way at work. Being safe his will pay for itself many times over.

Another type of risk is using your signature. Please know that your signature is your word. Putting your signature on paper means that you have read and understood and will do what the paper says. There is no getting away with I did not know. You must take time, read carefully and ask when you do not understand. Your manager and the HR function are there to help you understand what you are signing up for.

Background Summary

The second chapter is done. You know that your background is important. Knowing this is important to me. I want you to be safe and work where you are best suited.

Your manager might not know what he/she does not know. Please help them to help you. If you end up losing your job because you did not communicate your different background, schooling or exposure level, I would have failed with this book, and that I do not want for you or me. Please communicate.

Getting the Job

This book deals with "Work for Beginners." Now we get to the meat of the book.

Buckle in for the ride.

Getting a job is job number 1.

Job hunting is what most of us do at some stage of our lives.

Keep your eyes open. Wide open.

Look in newspapers - even if it is in the library or restaurant.

Look on job seeking website.

Register with Temporary Employment Services - the new name for Labour Brokers. These services can be the difference between getting that first job and sitting next to the road waiting for an opportunity. Remember, having work experience on your CV is important and proves that you can work.

The difficulty of finding a job is that you must sell yourself. Many of us have been taught not to sell ourselves. You must stand out and get the opportunity to get the job. Just be honest. Do not get chased out of the interview, although most interviewers are not as bad as I used to be, not even me.

So, let's get started.

CV

You can find plenty of advice on CV's and the contents of a CV on the Internet.

Curriculum Vitae - Story of your Life.

Tell the story of your work life in as short as possible way.

Some items are standard:

Name

Address

Contact Details

ID Number

Schooling

Further Education

Interests

Job Experience

Copy of Qualifications

Transcripts

Copy of ID book/card

Copy of Driver's license

Make sure the CV looks professional and has no spelling errors. I have never seen a handwritten CV. Maybe that would not be a bad thing. Either way, make sure you have plenty of copies of your CV. Do not be surprised if you need more than twenty before you get an interview - not a job, yet.

Some other less familiar items on a CV will be helpful. A personal mission statement – who are you and where are you in your life/career. Where do you want to be? List your skills as you have applied them. List skills you have used at charities or at school, for example planning a pageant, school play, running a soup kitchen.

You can set up your CV yourself or ask someone else to help you. If you are going to an interview with friends and you make use of the same service provider to create your CV's, make sure the service provider does a good job changing the details to reflect your details. The last thing you want is for someone like me to sit in the interview and remember that I have seen this CV format before and read this set of interests before. People take the path of least resistance and will not give you what you need if they can get away with it and make money. If you pay for it, it must be worth it. Proofread what you get - learn to be critical.

Be yourself in your CV.

In addition to the CV, you need a customised cover letter for every specific job opportunity. You can use a generic cover letter if you have a "cold call" - an unsolicited entry of your CV. If you are applying to a specific company, make sure you stand out and explain why you are the right person for the job. As indicated above you might have a low hit rate - less than one job interview out of twenty CV's handed out. Make sure you give yourself the best chance of being invited for an interview.

Interview

Go to the toilet before the interview, so that you do not interrupt your interview with a bathroom break. There is an exception mentioned later in this section.

Be on time.

Dress appropriately.

Drink something before going in, so that you can talk clearly without your tongue glued to the top of your mouth.

Be nervous, but don't show it.

In most interviews, you start by telling the interview panel who you are, so prepare that short statement in a clear way. Highlight what you have done and can contribute to the company.

Traditional interviews then move onto getting answers from you on standard prepared questions to test your knowledge and your fit to the job description. In my view, these interviews have their place, but as was described in the "Different Backgrounds" chapter you might not have had the required exposure to be able to answer the questions yet and still be a good candidate for the job.

Which way do you turn the tap to close the water at the water basin? Clockwise, or counterclockwise? Now is a good time for that bathroom break. In one job we had continued problems with employees closing taps that should be opened or not opening taps because they think the tap is already open - they did not know which way to turn the handle to close the tap. As part of the interview for this position, we asked candidates to tell us which way to turn the tap to close the water flow. Simple, yet important.

Another interview methodology abandons the "technical" questions and asks STAR questions. You are required to tell a story of a Situation you had to deal with, what the Task was, what Action you took and what the Result was. These stories tell me more about you and how you handle situations - not that you know how I expect you to answer the questions. This interview type also facilitates a test of whether you would be a cultural fit to the company. More on this later, since this is as important to the company as it is to you.

Medical

If you cannot hear or see properly, you will not work in my plant. Done. You need good hearing and good sight to be aware of your surroundings and the dangers that might be approaching you. I would rather not employ you than let you go later because you are a danger to yourself and others in your surroundings.

Please note that there are employment opportunities for people with disability and these opportunities should be pursued. Do not despair, lie and be caught out. Your safety is my concern, in addition to your ability to get a job.

Keep yourself at least moderately fit. As part of the process of entering the company as an employee, you will have to undergo an entrance medical exam. Should the doctor find you "unfit for work", your chances of working at that company has dropped to zero. Don't let that happen.

Often you do not know how healthy you are. So, visit the clinic and get an assessment of your lung function, eyesight and hearing as a minimum. Other conditions will not necessarily be known to you. The other conditions must be disclosed as early as possible - asthma as an example. The doctor often has a job-man specification that describes the physical effort and the environment in which you will be working and can establish whether you are acceptable for the position.

Again, do not despair. There are environments in which you can find work.

Summary of Getting the Job

So, you have handed out what feels like hundreds of copies of your CV. You have gone to endless interviews. You have seen plenty of managers, some friendly, some less so. You have felt confident and dismayed many times. Finally, a company offers you a job. You want to take it immediately; you need the money.

The company wants you.

Wait.

First, evaluate the job and the company.

Do you want the company?

Evaluate the Job

Cultures differ from country to country and for groups within the countries. Even families have different cultures.

The same is true of companies.

Culture is not always written down and is not easy to interpret from outside of the company. You must do your best though. You must know how well you will fit into the company. If the company cannot accommodate your needs, you will not be happy at the company.

Devout Christians might object to working on Saturdays (same for Jews) or Sundays. Muslims might object to not being given the opportunity to pray at their designated prayer times because of a continuous operation that they must always monitor. Other religious fasts might reduce your ability to perform manual labour because you are too weak during those times. Do not compromise your non-negotiables.

Can you do this?

The first obvious question is whether you think you can do the job. You have already convinced the interviewers that you can do the job. Maybe they were desperate to fill the position and decided to risk it. Maybe they feel that the only criteria are that you are available, have the minimum qualification, and ability to communicate. This short-sightedness should not be yours, though.

Look at the job description again, do you understand what

the company expects of you. Ask for a tour of the plant - this shows your commitment to the interview process. The tour also gives you the much-needed exposure talked about earlier in the book. During the tour, ask questions. See who else is working there. Can you do the job?

Do the people look happy? Are the people doing what you can see yourself doing? Do they greet the manager walking with you, or are they eyeing him? Learn to read the room as they say. Is there a mutual respect culture or a fear culture?

A smile.

A positive greeting.

Turned backs.

Raised voices.

Excitement.

Lack of excitement.

Be aware of your surroundings. Are there smells or dust that you think you will not be able to handle? Is there heat that you might not be able to tolerate?

Often you will not have to ask for a tour of the plant; the managers will include you on a plant tour. Show the necessary curiosity and ask questions. When your eyes light up, and the manager sees interest on your face, chances are you will have the job, AND you will fit.

Do you want to do this?

My uncle always said that the test of whether the job is for you is whether, if someone wakes you up at 03:00 in the morning you would happily jump out of bed and do the job. I have been tested many times at various times between 12:00 and 07:00 - even once with a fire in the plant, so I know I was in the right place.

The question is whether you think you will be in the right place?

How important are weekends with the family? If your answer is "very important", you will not fit into a schedule where you will see the family on both the Saturday and Sunday once in six weeks.

Are you able to stay up late? If not, night shift will be difficult for you. For that matter, if you find it difficult to wake up at the crack of dawn, early morning shift will also be difficult for you, as the misery of going to school early.

Time off work is not the only factor to consider but surely is very important.

Likewise, if the work entails hard manual labour and you cannot lift a 20 kg bag, you will not last a day of lifting 40 kg bags minute in and minute out.

Maybe you go insane doing the same thing all day long; then a monotonous job is not for you.

Maybe you need to see a computer screen every couple of minutes - then an administrative job is more to your liking than an assembly line job.

You are in control! You make the decision. You might think you do not have a choice, and often you have plenty of excuses to feel that way, but you do have a choice. Make a choice. Be the worker you want to be.

Are you willing to live with the Salary Package?

Money, Money, Money!

You need to get enough money to earn a living, even if you are passionate about what you do. When you find a job that allows you to live your purpose, you are truly blessed.

You need to decide how much money you need to "earn a living". You, and only you know your circumstances. You know how much your roof costs, how much your phone costs, how much your food costs, how much your entertainment costs. You might have other expenses like debt, or school fees for siblings, hospital costs for your ailing mother. Many others. Do not forget the transport cost of getting to work and taking food with you or buying food from the canteen.

At the very least you want the salary to cover the items listed above, as it pertains to you. Only then can you move forward and build a stable financial future for yourself. More on this later, when I end up on a philosophical note.

For now, we will look at some of the components of your income. Your pay should be straightforward, but many times it is not. Bear with me.

The important thing is the amount of money you know

you will take home at the end of the month. I think of this as the amount of bread I will be able to buy for the hours I spent at work.

Base Salary

When you sign on the dotted line, you sign that you are happy with the remuneration the company has offered you. Whether this is true or not. Later you might find that others are getting paid more than you are - there might be many legitimate reasons for the difference in pay - the long and the short of it is that you were happy to sign to work for that amount of money. That's why in the previous section I invited you to weigh up the costs and the benefits and know whether you can earn a living in this job.

Equal pay for equal work!

Not so much.

The company will pay you the wage/salary for which you signed.

Your base salary might be a singular amount before taking tax into account. Often, you are offered an hourly rate with a commitment to make use of your time for a certain number of hours per week, if everything goes as planned. At times you might be working more hours, and at times you might be working fewer hours.

The company might pay your wage weekly or monthly. Should you be paid weekly, you have the challenge of making sure you do not spend the money before your rent, and other monthly expenses become due. Therefore, many companies pay even hour paid workers monthly.

Do not underestimate the amount of tax you will be paying. You pay the government.

In an ideal world, you will be able to earn a living on this basic salary only. This section of your pay is the most secure. Even when you try to get a cell phone contract, this is the part the mobile service provider uses to assess affordability. The same applies when you want to buy furniture on credit. Please note, as stated above, sometimes not even this part of your salary is secure.

The other items are "bonuses", and often these "bonuses" are the items that keep you alive, but you should not commit to spending these "bonuses". The best thing would be to use these "bonuses" to save for rainy days. I know this sounds very difficult and is difficult, but this is my strong opinion, and you are free not to follow this recommendation - know that not following this advice might come at a cost.

You will eventually need the money for:

When you do lose this job for whatever reason - companies close or "shed jobs" at an alarming rate.

When you want to study.

When you want furniture or a smartphone.

When you are ill.

When a loved one is ill.

When you get married.

When you get children.

When you retire.

Many other reasons.

Let's look at other ways the company will give you money, sometimes.

Allowances

You might get a car allowance, but these are few and far between, and the company should ideally reserve car allowances for someone who travels on behalf of the company with their private vehicle. Car allowances used to give some tax benefit, but not anymore. You do get some money back if you indeed travelled on behalf of the company, but it does not make money. The company cannot guarantee this allowance, for example, if you have a job that requires travelling and your responsibilities change you might no longer get the car allowance, remember what I said earlier.

Many people think of work taking place between 9 and 5 - more accurately 08:00 and 16:30, or 07:15 and 16:30, or 07:00 and 16:30.

Shift work comes in different shapes and sizes. From Monday to Friday. From Monday to Sunday. Twelve hours per day, eight hours per day, two shifts of twelve hours per day, two shifts of eight hours, three shifts of twelve hours and a blend of all the shifts.

When you work shifts, there is usually some arrangement to make up for the "inconvenience" of being at work when "normal" people would not be at work. Whatever normal means.

Generally, the allowance might take the form of 8 % for those starting work in the afternoon and 12 % for those starting work at night.

Shift allowance is only applicable when you work the applicable shifts.

The company might pay you based on actual hours worked and the commensurate allowance or may choose to be merciful and pay you an average allowance so that your take-home pay stays relatively constant from month to month. The allowance earned in a month can vary significantly from month to month depending on where you are in your shift cycle and which allowances are due to you. Someone might work night shift in the first week, afternoon shift in the next week and morning shift in the third work and end the month at night shift again - Jackpot! The next month will not be so generous with only one week of night shift in the month.

Another allowance is a standby allowance. The company will sometime pay standby allowances when you need to be available to the company at times you do not need to be on the company premises. You cannot have a drink. You cannot go to a far-off destination. You need to stay close to work and be available on the phone and get to work soon after you are called to be available. The company pays you for the inconvenience.

Another allowance is a stand-in allowance, which is worth its weight in gold. After you have established yourself in your appointed position and can do the job, work on getting to know some of the next level jobs. You benefit from gaining more exposure. You get the training. You get to be available for a possible promotion. When you stand-in for a person in a higher position than yourself, you might get a stand-in allowance. Be the person to step into the next person's shoes when they go on leave. The company benefits, and you benefit.

The allowances are not a sure thing. Again, with the soapbox. The allowances can change when your working hours change! Changes in working hours can happen for many reasons - possibly a promotion to a position which pays a higher basic salary but has no allowance. You give up the promotion because you "take home less money", but if you saw the allowances as "bonus money" you would rather take the promotion and the next one and the next one and . . . CEO?

Overtime

From time to time the company will need more working hours per week than originally agreed with you. The extra hours will, however, not justify a different shift system, this means the same number of people work more hours to make sure that customers get what they need when they need it - hopefully at a higher price to the company.

The company reimburses these extra hours at a different rate. You might get paid 33 % extra, 50 % extra, or 100 % extra, OR you might be given time off at a later stage to make up for the extra time worked. The time off might be at a time when the company does not need your services for as long as they had agreed on this with you.

So, you see, overtime is not a given! Do not fall into the trap of buying bread with the overtime money - next month you might not have enough money for your new normal amount of bread.

Overtime is often needed when someone else goes on leave, and the gaps in the shift need to be filled by the employees staying behind to continue to run the plant.

Keep track of your overtime. Make notes. Your manager does not want to short-change you, and the payroll function does not want to pay you less than you worked for, but the system might be slow in catching up with what you are owed.

Leave

Leave, glorious leave. Leave is not to be confused with all the time you had off at school or the tertiary institution. You will need the break.

Please use the break to rest - do something completely different, even if it is to help build a home for your grandmother.

How and when you take leave will be different from employer to employer and can become very complicated. An easy methodology is to work the first year without going on leave and taking all the leave you built up in that year sometime during the next six months. One nice long break!

Note, again, that the company might have busy and slow

periods and might ask you to take your leave during the slow periods so that they do not have too much working capacity in that period - beats working short time! Also, the company might have what is called a shutdown. A shutdown is a period when the plant stops producing, and the engineering function focuses on maintenance or improvement projects. During this time, unless the company needs some extra cleaners (assuming that you are not the cleaner) as an example, you will not be required to be at work, so you must take your leave then. Plan. Ask if, and when there will be shutdowns and what the rules are.

Your leave is yours but know you might not have the luxury to take leave when you want to. If, for example, you need leave for your honeymoon plan this in advance and discuss this with your manager and fellow employees.

Pension

The company might contribute to a retirement fund. That is about it.

The days of companies paying you a salary after your retirement is mostly long gone. You must make your arrangements to have money after your retirement. The money you and the company pay into the retirement fund will be available to you when you retire to do as you please, subject to government regulations.

Retirement, usually at 65 years old, is probably a long way off for you. Know, that the sooner you start contributing to your retirement the better. There is no time like now. You will be sorry if you do not contribute as soon as now, not when you can, now!

Also, when you lose your job, you will be able to get hold of your retirement fund. The government wants to protect you against yourself and say that you do not have access to the money, yet. Good on them, in this regard. Please do not take the money and waste it - any use will be a waste.

Remember, I wrote earlier about the shareholder(s) of the company - you might have become a shareholder of your company - even if it is indirectly. What is good for the company is good for you too.

The forced retirement fund contribution is a good thing, but your take-home pay will be less. You should evaluate the influence of the retirement fund contribution when comparing different jobs. The benefits are important and will be valuable in the long run, but in the short run, you will have less money for bread. You might need to live off less bread now that you have all of these "benefits".

Medical

You and the company might be making contributions to a medical aid scheme and reduces the take-home pay.

This area is also full of pitfalls. Remember, your needs will change over time. As a young healthy adult, you will need less cover than a married person.

Read and read and get a magnifying glass and read all the fine print. Do as much as you can to understand the benefits – what the scheme covers and what not.

For example, as a first-time contributor to a medical aid scheme you might have a three-month waiting period before going to the doctor, or even worse a twelve-month waiting period before you have maternity benefits.

Be careful not to abuse the medical aid scheme, but get done what needs to get done. If you have any health problems, that does not affect your ability to do your work, get them fixed. Remember that you cannot get a cosmetic nose job and be off work for weeks!

In many cases part of the hazards of working in a plant environment, as an example, is exposure to noise. Custom made hearing protection will be worth it, and some medical aid schemes pay for the hearing protection.

Other Benefits

There might be other added benefits from working for the company. Discounted food at the canteen, which is cheaper than restaurant food, but more expensive than fruit and sandwiches brought from home. Leftovers from dinner also come in handy.

Some companies offer access to sports clubs or gyms at ridiculous prices. Don't injure yourself, though. You have an obligation towards yourself and the company to be in good health.

You might choose the current company as your employer because the company is close to home, which reduces your transport cost, or you have friends who already work in the plant. Remember this is not a social club, you are at work to work.

You might want to work where your father or uncle or

aunt works. Working with family might be against company policy - check with the human resources function before losing your job for non-disclosure at a later stage. Nepotism is a dangerous game.

Summary of Job Evaluation

Now you know how to evaluate yourself and the job you are considering. You know whether you want the job or not. Sign on the dotted line. The hard work starts.

Keeping the Job

You have spent a lot of time job hunting.

Surprise!

The hard work is to keep the job.

There is only one way to keep the job. Get the desired results.

To consistently get the desired results you must show commitment.

The concept of getting the desired results applies to all levels within the company. From the bottom to the top. Results are what counts.

Near the bottom of the "food chain" your ability to control the results creatively is limited. You follow orders, and the orders get the company results, gets you results.

Therefore, you must follow the rules.

Before you can follow the rules, you must know what the rules are.

Therefore, listen and ask questions. Get to know the rules.

Respect the induction process. To many, this might seem like a waste of time, but this is the time you get to know the culture of the company better - and this in a safe environment.

The upside of induction within a group is that you might find a group of friends with whom you will have a connection for a long time. And this is with people from different functions.

Let me hurry up before you lose interest in reading this book to completion.

Timekeeping

Timekeeping is not valued as it used to be valued.

Work is not school; it is not a church, it is not the movies. You are on time, or you are out. Done. The work needs to get done. Often there will be an opening meeting. You want to get the data at these meetings. You want to know how the team did. You want to know how you did. You want to hear what you have to do in the day. You want to know what has changed. You want to know what there is to learn. Be there on time. Do not miss anything.

The work must continue as planned. Do not be the one to confuse your manager - is this person going to pitch up for work or not.

I start with timekeeping because everything starts with timekeeping.

Good timekeeping is the basis of all discipline. If you are not on time, chances are you're your manager will not consider you for further training, nor for promotions, your managers will not see you as a good employee. You want to stay in everyone's good books. Be reliable. Be on time.

Later I will discuss Industrial Relations. Know that the base concept is progressive discipline. Progressive discipline means that on day one you are late, you get a verbal warning. On day two you are late, you get a written warning. On day three you are late, you get a final written warning. On day four you are late; the company dismisses you for poor time keeping - you lose your job. All within the law and you do not have legal recourse. Goodbye. All the hard work of getting a job gone. Do not be late.

Arranging Transport

As part of being on time, you want to make sure you plan your commute. Make sure you have safe and reliable transport. Do not be caught out, not even once. If it does happen, evaluate what went wrong and make sure you get to work safely and on time.

Some employees make it a point to aim to be early for work by as much as two hours. I am not asking you to be that early. Remember the story about the heroes. You might have a massively uncomfortable time to get to work. Let it be worth it.

Safe and reliable transport will mean different things to different people; hence the background story is important. Get to grips with your reality. If you have transport arrangements with someone else, mention this to your managers so that they know how they can move you from one shift to another. If they move you away from your transport arrangements and you did not tell them of your arrangements, you will have to tell them, which will cause a lot of rework of a proper plan - don't cause hassles, communicate in time. If your transport is in jeopardy, please take the time to communicate this to your managers, despite fearing the rework - you need to be on time, so make sure you can be on time.

Be aware of what is happening in the area you live in. There might be protests or other strikes, and you might not be able to get to work. Try to get to work. Do not risk your life. If you tried and fear for your life, let your manager know that you are unable to get to work and explain why you are not able to get to work. If others made it, learn from them. Again, you weigh up the risks you are willing to take. Have evidence of why you are unable to reach the company so that you do not fall prey to progressive discipline.

Shift Arrangements

I have mentioned the impact of shifts on your pocket earlier. I have mentioned that you need to evaluate the impact of the time you are supposed to be at work on your social and family life. Think about it again.

You must learn how to deal with shifts.

Transport is in the bag.

Make sure that you can eat and sleep in peace. Remember, others do not know you are sleeping to get to work at night. Be ready to have a poor day's sleep. And prevent it from happening again.

Please make sure you stay away from the wrong food and drink - energy drinks. You might think you need these to get you through the night. Change your routines so that you are strong no matter when you need to be at work. Be healthy.

Should you need advice, speak to your occupational health officers - the nurse. Find out what you can do. Make sure your room is dark, not too hot, not too cold and as quiet as you can have it.

You might find yourself in a situation where you come from work at 18:00 and need to be back at work the next morning before 05:45 AND your travel time is two hours for both directions, leaving you eight hours to relax, cook, eat, sleep, bathe and the rest. Be prepared. The time pressure is rough. Make sure you plan your food and sleep properly.

On the Job Training

As mentioned earlier, the circle of life makes sure that you are at the bottom often.

You might think you know a thing or two but know that you must start at the bottom again.

Walk into the job as though you know nothing. Learn what you need to know as quickly as possible. Become productive only when you are sure you know how to do what you need to do and do it safely while getting the results.

On the job training is important. Even something as mundane as filing might trip you up. You might think that you should file in alphabetical order, but the company policy is to file according to the nature of the supplier's product they sell to the company.

Be willing to learn.

No matter what your qualification, you have not been at this company before and chances are you have not been in this industry before, so you start at the beginning, the bottom and work your way up to being knowledgeable.

Learn at the pace the company allows you to learn. Use this time as an opportunity to learn how things work.

Training and the OHS Act

The Occupational Health and Safety Act requires that the company trains you in your duties. Therefore, the company and you have a duty to each other to make sure you only perform duties you are trained to do. Nothing more and hopefully nothing less.

I know you are eager to please. I know you are eager to start getting results.

No result is worth your life. No result is worth your job.

People have been dismissed for quickly climbing onto a forklift truck and helping. Their heart was in the right place. They wanted to help. They wanted to solve a problem on behalf of the company. BUT they were not trained. They lost their job. Do not let this be you.

To comply with the Occupational Health and Safety Act, the company must give you a Works Instruction or Safe Operating Procedure or Standard Operating Procedure that describes what you need to do and how to do it safely. You might get other training material as well. Also, the company must give you a risk assessment - a document detailing the risk of doing the job and how the company mitigates these risks. Then there must be proof that the company has trained you in these documents.

Next, you must show that you have worked under the supervision of a competent person and become adept at doing the task. I always say, if the person supervising you cannot touch your shoulder you are not being supervised. If that person goes to the loo, you stop.

There must be a task observation, where the manager or some other subject matter expert (possibly from the training function) observes you doing the task as trained to do so - this step must be repeated several times during your career.

The company also needs to prove that they have taken

disciplinary steps - remember progressive discipline - to make sure you always adhere to the safety requirements of the task.

You have a grasp of one task. Next step, please.

Gaining Competence

Your job at the company will inevitably consist of several tasks. Work at the pace allowed at the company and allowed by your abilities and learn each task to the satisfaction of the manager or trainer. Build up your competence in your job.

At times the needs of the company will bring your progress to a standstill. You might have learned a single task, which allows you to perform those tasks safely and help the company through a busy period. Do not allow what is temporary to become permanent. As soon as the "crisis" is gone, ask to progress with the rest of your tasks.

Become familiar with as many tasks as possible. Become trained in all the tasks for your job. Being multi-skilled will ensure that you are as useful and versatile as you are intended to be.

Some managers might see you as a machine, as a flesh and bone piece of equipment that the company can easily replace with a metal machine. The biggest difference between you and a machine is that you can do infinitely more tasks than a machine that has been built and programmed to perform a singular task in one way.

Make sure you are more than a machine.

Once you have gained the competency in your job, gain

proficiency. What do I mean? Work on doing the job at more than the minimum level required, aim for the professional level the company needs. Remember, you are the one who touches the machine, do the tasks every day, be the specialist. Contribute ideas of how to make the process safer, better. You will also benefit, eventually - even if it only gives you a good STAR story to tell in your next interview.

So, start again, at the bottom.

Asking for the next Step

Some people can perform one set of tasks well. Nothing else. That's OK. Be the backbone of the company - never allow yourself to be merely a machine, though.

Be willing to start at the bottom again.

Volunteer to learn the tasks for the next step, the next level or at the same level. Make sure you have proven yourself in your current job first, though. The more you know, the better your chances of getting promoted to the next level in the hierarchy.

You might even be lucky and be given an opportunity in another department, allowing you to see other managers and other implementations of the company policy. Don't expect the same amount of respect though. You must earn it, again.

Once you are satisfied, be satisfied.

If you are still not satisfied, move on to the next step.

Remember this is your first or close to your first job. There might be more in you. Only you will know when you have reached your limit. If there is a limit imposed on you, evaluate life. Is it that you think too much of yourself, then work on yourself. Is it that the company does not have anywhere else for you to go, then move out. Is it that a person is blocking your progress, then handle that situation through the hierarchy and human resources function.

Attitude

You know that you can perform the tasks required to do the job.

You can also see the path to the top.

Be patient.

Do not rush onto the next level, yet.

Are you as proficient in your current job as you can be?

Have you built the trust relationship with your managers you need to move onto the next level?

Have you proven yourself?

Have you obtained results?

Have you grown in the culture of the company?

Do you have the required respect and loyalty?

Are you working diligently?

Be careful. Everything you do and say will be used against you. In one way or another what you do is recorded and will be used to make decisions regarding your future.

Respect and Loyalty

You can be happy to have a job.

What? Be happy with doing this? You must be kidding?

"You can be happy to have a job" can be interpreted in many ways. The truth is that many people do not have a job. Hence the statement is true. The statement should never be used to intimidate you into doing something you have not been trained to do. The statement should never be used to make you do something you cannot do. The statement should never be used to keep you in your place.

So, what should your attitude towards work be?

Respect, loyalty and diligence.

Do what you do, to the best of your ability, always. Know what the company expects of you and do it well.

The ultimate example of loyalty is probably a dog. The dog is part of the household pride. The dog shows love and commitment, no matter how you treat it. The dog accepts its lot in life.

You are not a dog.

So how should you be respectful, loyal and diligent?

Respect and Loyalty for the Job

Be thankful you have a job. Really. Being thankful will inform your attitude in the best way possible.

Know that you contribute to the success of the company and the company contributes, even if only with a wage/salary, to your success.

Having a job gives you so much more than just money. The job gives you things only you can understand because of your unique background.

The company gives you money to perform some tasks in a specific safe way. Do them.

Hopefully, you get more than that.

Hopefully, you get to be part of something bigger. You get to build the economy, make people's houses better, make their offices better, make their transport better, give them the ability to be transported. See the bigger picture. Yes, there might be very little you can get from your job, and it might just be what it is but know that it is important to you.

Be available. Be available to do what needs to be done when it needs to be done. If overtime is required, be the one to volunteer for the overtime. If something different needs to be done, do that - after being trained.

If someone from outside wants to badmouth your company, remember it is your company. What they say about the company they are saying about you. If you agree with what others are saying and this clashes with who you are, move on. Otherwise, stand up for yourself and your company - set the record straight.

Do not allow peer pressure to make you think you are working for a bad company with poor managers – you chose to work for the company, remember.

Respect and loyalty to Your Manager

Good managers should be the only type of manager you meet at work. Having good managers is, however not always the case.

Good managers make sure you have what you need to perform. They facilitate you achieving your results. They make sure the equipment is in working order, that the raw materials are available, that you know what you need to do during the shift and that you know how to do your job.

Take what you get. To some extent.

If you can still perform - achieve results - accept the person for who he/she is. Your manager might need a good right hand, be that good right hand if you fit the bill.

If you cannot perform, or your safety is in danger, or your manager is abusing you, do something. Talk to the manager, then the manager's superior, then to the next level. Get human resources involved. Get the trade union shop steward involved. Do not lose your job, though. Do what you do with respect.

Value mentors. Don't expect them.

In addition to the bare minimum, you might find a manager who takes you under his/her wing and shows you the ropes in a more profound way than just the mechanics of the job. They might see something in you that you see in yourself or missed in yourself.

Learn when conflict is appropriate. The answer is, nearly never. When faced with a difficult command, first comply and then appropriately raise your grievance, later. Full-blown conflict will probably reflect badly on you, rather than the offending manager. Do not make impulsive decisions.

Take what you get. Run with it. Be thankful. Use the opportunity to learn. Learn the job. Learn how to work with people. How to plan. How to solve problems. How to contribute more to the success of everyone involved in the company. All of this helps you prepare for your next job – the future is in your hand.

Respect and loyalty for Yourself

Take the time to get to know yourself. Know what is important to you. Know what your limits are - know what is legal/illegal, ethical and moral according to your interpretation and that of your family.

You have obligations to the company.

You also have obligations towards yourself and to those you love.

Understand those obligations.

Fill your needs.

Fill the needs of your loved ones.

You are not a robot. You do have needs. You have psychological, physical, mental and spiritual needs.

Set boundaries.

Be true to yourself.

Communicate what you are experiencing. At times you will need to look after a sick loved one because there is no one else to do so. You might need time off, or you will not be able to work overtime, then explain your circumstances and do what you need to do with a clear conscience.

You are entitled to fair treatment, make sure you are treated fairly.

A clear sign that you respect yourself is that you have clean clothes without holes and that your shoes are shiny. Do the small things, and the big things will take care of themselves, with some effort.

Respect and loyalty for Fellow Employees

Dealing with fellow employees can be painful. You don't know what to do.

Cover their arses.

Stab them in the back.

Those seem to be the only two options.

Never put your job in jeopardy.

Look after your fellow employees as far as you can. Plan, with your manager, to facilitate extra training where extra training is required but do not allow unsafe acts to continue. No job is worth someone's life. Even the most dangerous jobs can be done safely when the risks are understood.

Never commit fraud on behalf of a fellow employee. Do not clock in for them. Do not complete forms for them. Do not lie to your manager. You will be caught out. You might lose your job. Don't do the crime if you cannot pay the time.

Being kind is cruel.

If someone cannot do the job, let the manager handle the situation. They should be able to find another opportunity for your fellow employee to perform at work.

If you can help, help. If you can explain differently, explain the work so that the other employees understand the work. If the person is not strong enough to do the work day in and day out, find a better way of doing the work so that everyone can benefit from the better way.

Be true to yourself.

Diligence

Diligence means you work as hard as you can for as long as you can as good as you can.

You might be enticed to do more, don't. If you continually push yourself beyond your limits, your health and safety will suffer. Pushing your boundaries from time to time makes you stronger but be smart about it.

Do your tasks to the best of your abilities with the tools you have. If something is not right, fix it. Be part of the solution. Speak up and highlight the problem. Improve the situation for everyone.

Safe Work

You have been trained to perform the tasks safely. Safely do them.

Work safely.

Do not take chances.

Do make contributions to a safer environment.

Report unsafe acts - when someone does something in a way that is unsafe. For example, people taking a chance and doing the work without the agreed personal protective equipment (PPE). Remember the risk assessments you did. The area might be noisy. The company cannot reduce the noise because the process is inherently noisy. The company gives you hearing protection - earplugs. These are uncomfortable, especially when you are sweating. Your fellow worker regularly works without his earplugs. Report this. If you don't, your friend might end up with occupational deafness and need hearing aids to hear his/her grandchildren play with each other. Know that what you don't do today will influence your quality of life later.

Report unsafe conditions - when something is not as safe as it could be. There might be an oil leak. This oil leak might be allowed to grow until someone slips on this leak. The tripping might be funny in the moment, but no joke when your fellow worker ends up in the hospital with a concussion. All this because you did not report the leak. Take the time and look after the plant, and yourself.

Hard Work

Work hard.

At the end of the day, this is all that counts. Have you continually worked hard? Have you consistently achieved the results you were expected to achieve?

In many cases the hard work is physically hard work, other times it is intellectually hard work.

No matter what form the hard work takes, only you can do it. No one else can perform the work on your behalf.

Do what is expected of you, always.

Look after yourself.

Eat well.

Sleep well.

Do some exercise - even if it is only to warm up before the day's physical work.

When you are ill, make a judgment call. If you cannot work safely, stay at home and get better as soon as possible, otherwise get up and go to work.

You are your means to an end. If your body and mind cannot perform, you will not earn a living.

Take the breaks you are entitled to take. Take your leave. You are entitled to your leave. Enjoy your leave.

Take the breaks you are entitled to take. Again? Yes, again. Many shift systems give you some relatively large breaks between your stints at work. Use these breaks to recharge - you do not always know when the company will expect you to work overtime. Do not find other ways to supplement your income which limit your ability to rest and come back strong. There is nothing wrong with having a side hustle or studying during your breaks. Just do not be in contravention of the company policies. Also, don't be tired when you go back to work.

Smart Work

Don't be the fast food cashier asking whether you want cheese on your cheeseburger.

Be aware of what you are doing. Ask yourself whether you are there in the moment. Be at work with your body and mind. Don't just be hands and feet and a back - be a brain.

See what you are doing and think of how you can make things better. Better for yourself and others. At the very least look out for ways of doing things safer every day.

Make sure you can put the company, and thereby you, in a better position than you were yesterday.

Companies often have improvement projects, take part in these. Speak up. You are the one who touches the raw materials, equipment and the products; you know best what is happening - contribute and take pride in the results.

Summary of Keeping the Job

Good. You have found a job you roughly like and you are ready to work. You are trained to work. You know how to work safely. You know how to get the results.

Management will always expect you to work faster, better with less.

Keep the job; please keep the job by working safe, hard and smart.

Your Rights

You have rights.

Remember the entitlement problem I wrote about earlier. Do not fall into the entitlement trap. Know your rights. Temper your expectations.

There is a common refrain: "Justice delayed is Justice denied." Don't fall into the trap of populism. All justice takes time; you must be persistent.

The employer and employee are in a relationship with each other. This relationship is consensual. You signed on the dotted line. I always said, "your arse is grass, and I am the lawn mower." Indicating that you have agreed to work, and I will give you work to do.

The relationship might go well - happy days.

The relationship might not go so well - oops!

The employer and the employee have rights, and at a minimum, these rights must be respected and obeyed.

I am not a lawyer. I am not an HR practitioner. I am not a Trade Unionist. These are the people you should turn to when things go wrong. I intend to give you a background of what rights you have and how these rights apply to you. I am a South African - born and bred. Therefore, the legislation I mention is South African legislation; there are equivalent legal documents in other countries, and you should consult them. You will get a basic picture of what you can expect.

Constitution

The Constitution forms the basis of all laws in South Africa.

No law may be put in place (promulgated) unless the lawmakers test the law against the constitution. No law may infringe on any rights described and given to a South African as described in the constitution.

Much of the constitution deals with how Government is set up and what the hierarchy of the government is. You might be interested in this since it sheds light on what the newspapers say.

Don't fall into the trap of referring to the constitution when it comes to your rights. The constitution is a general document detailing the "Bill of Rights." Also, remember that your right to exercise your rights may never harm your fellow employees.

The section in the constitution that describes the labour relation is as follows:

23. Labour relations.--

(1) Everyone has the right to fair labour practices.

(2) Every worker has the right-

(a) to form and join a trade union;

(b) to participate in the activities and programmes of a trade union; and

(c) to strike.

(3) Every employer has the right-

(a) to form and join an employers' organisation; and

(b) to participate in the activities and programmes of an employers' organisation.

(4) Every trade union and every employers' organisation has the right-

(a) to determine its own administration, programmes and activities;

(b) to organise; and

(c) to form and join a federation.

(5) Every trade union, employers' organisation and employer has the right to engage in collective bargaining. National legislation may be enacted to regulate collective bargaining. To the extent that the legislation may limit a right in this Chapter, the limitation must comply with section 36 (1).

(6) National legislation may recognise union security arrangements contained in collective agreements. To the extent that the legislation may limit a right in this Chapter, the limitation must comply with section 36 (1).

36. Limitation of rights.-

1) The rights in the Bill of Rights may be limited only in terms of law of general application to the extent that the limitation is reasonable and justifiable in an open and democratic society based on human dignity, equality and freedom, taking into account all relevant factors, including-

(a) the nature of the right;

(b) the importance of the purpose of the limitation;

(c) the nature and extent of the limitation;

(d) the relation between the limitation and its purpose; and

(e) less restrictive means to achieve the purpose.

As can be read above the constitution is a general document.

now that you may belong to a trade union.

Know that bargaining can take place and often takes place in a collective sense, in other words, a set of trade unions negotiate on behalf of an industry with the employers in the industry to determine some of the working conditions in that industry.

OHS Act

The workplace is not home.

No kidding.

A simple example would be our general view of what is a safe act. At home, we regularly use a chair to get something off the top of a cupboard. At work, this would be an unsafe act and an unsafe condition - as mentioned earlier.

The Occupational Health and Safety Act describes the employer and employee responsibility towards safety at work.

In short, make sure you are trained to do your tasks and only do the tasks you have been trained to do and only in the safe way you were taught to do them. If you do something you have not been trained to do, you are in trouble. If you do something differently from how the company trained you, you are in trouble. If you do not wear the protective clothing you were given or are expected to wear, you are in trouble.

Please, the Occupational Health and Safety Act is not there to be a punishment, it is there to protect you and make sure you go home in good health.

You will often want to do something, for the right reasons on behalf of the company, but not in a safe way. Do not do it. Your life is more important than doing something quickly. Make sure the company trains you. Done.

You can show yourself as willing and able by being trained as a first aider (someone who attends to injuries in the short term) or a safety representative. A safety representative talks to management about what the employees see in the workplace, what is done in an unsafe way (unsafe acts) and what can potentially cause injuries - unsafe conditions.

BCEA

The <u>Basic Conditions of Employment Act</u> describes the minimum conditions of employment. The company may give you more than what the BCEA prescribes, but not less.

Do yourself a favour and read through this forty-page document - the BCEA gives you plenty of food for thought. You will understand aspects of working life, which you might only learn the hard way over a long period, for example, your hours of work, lunch times, overtime, Sunday work and public holidays.

Your leave is also important since you need to take a break at some time. At times tragedy strikes and the act provides time off for burials, or to make sure you recover from an illness.

Most importantly, you must be able to understand how you are paid and by whom.

Unfortunately, your time at your employer of choice might come to an end - hopefully, a happy end. There are certain rules which apply when you and your employer part ways. Know your rights, and make sure you leave on good terms.

The Department of Labour is your friend as far as safety, and the application of the BCEA is concerned.

Labour Relations Act

The Labour Relations Act describes the formation of trade unions, employer organisations and bargaining councils and courts and many other issues. The document is 155 pages long and is there for you to read. The employer is supposed to have a summary available on a public notice board.

The essence of the Labour Relations Act is that you have rights, that are protected. You are not alone in your problems. You may approach different bodies/courts to help you when things go wrong, or when you want to negotiate your salary. Usually, after you have signed your employment contract, you are stuck with your salary/wage until increase time comes. This increase might be performance-based, based on plant-based negotiation or based on what happens at a central bargaining council. The LRA describes how to form a bargaining council.

A word on trade unions and your relationship with them. Trade unions are there to represent you as an employee. You have the right to choose a trade union. You have the right to vote for Shop Stewards - the employees who will represent the trade union on behalf of the company's employees when discussing matters of mutual interest. The shop stewards will be your first stop when you feel that your managers are not listening to you. You pay to be protected by the union, get your money's worth. If you are not happy with your shop stewards, remember you voted them into their positions and democracy has run its course. So, vote when you have the opportunity.

If, and only if, you feel that you can represent your fellow employees in a compassionate and level-headed way, make yourself available as a shop steward. Do not be seen as a glory hound. To not be seen as a troublemaker. Be seen as a leader, an influencer, if that is who you are.

Compensation for Injury on Duty

The [Compensation for Occupational Injuries and Diseases Act](#) is another form of protection you get for making the economy work. If you injure yourself at work, you must report the incident, even if you are macho. Do not take a chance. Any injury, no matter how small, can be infected and cause big problems in future. If you do not follow the rules of reporting the injury, you may lose the opportunity to be compensated. Do not take chances with your financial well-being.

If you injure yourself during the performance of your duties, the compensation fund will look after your medical bills. Remember that there is the Occupational Health and Safety Act. You cannot accidentally on purpose injure yourself and go on a paid holiday and be paid out for losses suffered. There is no such thing as a free meal. Please take note of the following provision in the act "22 3 (a) *If an accident is attributable to the serious and willful misconduct of the employee, no compensation shall be payable in terms of this Act*".

Please take note that a visit from the Department of Labour Inspector is not fun for anyone involved. You and your employer will need to prove that you have complied with all the safety precautions. You will be involved in a company investigation into the injury, and if the injury falls into a "reportable" category, you will also be part of the Department of Labour's investigation. This investigation will determine who was at fault. The department of labour might take a year to investigate, so keep a record of what happened and who saw what. You must protect yourself and know what happened.

Skills Development

The [Skills Development Levies Act](#) creates Sector Education and Training Authorities to make sure employees get skills. These skills development initiatives can come in the form of learnerships - remember I wrote about those opportunities earlier in the book.

Skills development is important. Government, society, the employers and you all benefit from gaining better skills. Skills development does not mean you can apply for a job and train as a doctor because you want to become a doctor. The skills development is strictly controlled to help the specific sector achieve what that sector believes it needs to be able to perform better as a sector. A better sector should result in better companies, which should result in better benefits for all employees.

EE

The [Employment Equity Act](#) aims to ensure that there is no discrimination on the basis of "*race, gender, sex, pregnancy, marital status, family responsibility, ethnic or social origin, colour, sexual orientation, age, disability, religion, HIV status, conscience, belief, political opinion, culture, language and birth.*"

If you feel that the company has discriminated against

you, you have certain options available to you.

Affirmative Action is also addressed specifically in the employment equity act and insists that *"affirmative action measures are measures designed to ensure that suitably qualified people of designated groups have equal employment opportunities and are equitably represented in all occupational categories and levels in the workforce of a designated employer."*

The company must have an employment equity plan and must report on the progress made in following this plan to government or suffer the consequences.

Summary of Rights

You are done with this highly important chapter. Please, please remember that you have rights and know your rights. With the rights come responsibilities. Take responsibility for your welfare, and if others threaten you, take them to task.

The law protects you.

All the laws in the whole world will make no difference if you have not made the right decisions for yourself. Do not start working for a company that will make you unhappy. Be civil. Remember the lessons your elders taught you and stick to them. Respect your manager. Talk to your manager. Communicate well. Be sure you have made your desires clear - your desire to be safe, your desire to be compensated correctly, your desire to be able to stand up for your rights, your desire to be compensated for an injury, your desire to acquire skills and your desire to be treated fairly.

Last Sage Advice

Please indulge me in these last pages to share some more out-on-a-limb sage advice. These points are important, and I do not want you to learn the hard way. Undoubtedly, you will see them as impossible dreams. You will see them as impossible as some of the financial advice I have sprinkled into the body of this book already. Please know, that you can choose not to heed my advice.

Look After your Finances

You are about to earn a wage/salary. Your first paycheck from this company might be your first pay ever. Or this might be a new employment opportunity, and you will get more money than in your previous job.

Remember, you have survived thus far, even if it is on the good graces of your family and friends.

If possible start your financial well-being on a good foot. Now is the best time. And for most of us, this is the last time.

Live a year behind - this means that you do not spend your salary. Yes, I expect you to work and get nothing for it! You do not know what will happen in the future. Money in the bank will help you cover your expenses when they are there, and necessary. Do not get a cell phone contract, do not buy new clothes, do not move into better living accommodation, do not eat more. All of this sounds crazy, I know. What you do not know is that if you do not do this now, you will never be able to do it.

So, what happens next year. Next year you get an increase if you are lucky. Then you start living on what you earned in your first year. So, you earned zero before landing the job, continue to live on zero, not your 1000 bucks a week for the first year. Then you get 1060 bucks in your second year. Live off 1000 bucks, not 1060 - save the 60 bucks. And so, magically, you have a good stash of cash for a rainy day, and believe me when it rains, it pours.

Discuss this with your family and friends. They need to understand why you are not living as you earn it. They must not force you to spend money now and have nothing later. They must not think you are abusing them or being selfish and stingy.

OK. OK. If you cannot live off zero, try at least to live off of half your initial salary and possibly continue in that way.

Budget

You will need to open a bank account if you do not already have a bank account.

The bank looks after your money and facilitates transactions on your behalf. One set of such transactions is bank fees. Beware. The bank fees could potentially wipe out a significant portion of your income. There is nothing wrong with banks who charge you high bank fees if you feel you get value for your money. Your choice of bank and bank account must suit your needs. Do not pay for something you will not need. Added benefits are not necessarily benefiting you in the short run.

You will also need to start budgeting. How much money will you save? Save as much as possible in the first year; then things become much easier.

A budget is a plan of how much money you expect to earn - remember allowances and overtime are not guaranteed income and need to be treated differently from you basic wage/salary. Use allowance and overtime to save for other luxury items and to make sure you have a good nest egg. You will never have as much money as you have now when you obtain a significant other and kids your money will become theirs, not yours.

The other side of a budget is the planned expenses. Do not plan to spend more than you know you will bring home every month. Do not make debt. You do not need the most recent cell phone or the most recent fashion accessory - you do not need a luxury vehicle; no matter how fancy it is. Food, housing, electricity, medicine, saving and other expenses. Plan. Budget. Live.

Don't make babies

Sex is for procreation not for recreation.

I am the father of two lovely daughters. I will not exchange them for all the wealth in the world. Therefore, as far as I am concerned kids are a good thing.

Unplanned kids can be heart-breaking for the mother, father, grandparents and eventually for the kids. If you cannot pay the time, do not do the crime. Kids eat up your income, no doubt. They will make you enter adulthood even faster than the job you just got, so watch out.

I have asked many people where babies come from, especially expectant parents. Almost no-one knows. Surprise!

A quick reminder, check that your medical aid scheme will cover the medical expenses of pregnancy and birth.

When the baby comes, forget all the above. Love them. Love yourself.

Lose the Booze

This is a difficult one. I am a teetotaller and hence do not know what it is like being drunk.

I have seen alcohol destroy lives, though.

If you pitch up for work under the influence of alcohol, you will unsafe and possibly face disciplinary action and possibly lose your job.

Being drunk also means you might have to pass on some valuable overtime.

Booze can also make you lose track of time and destroy your good timekeeping – this can create untold problems.

Lose the Booze before you lose your job.

Summary of this Book

Done. You have made it through the book, congratulations. Please practice what you have learnt. If you have not learnt anything, go back and read again.

Your work-life influences your happiness to a large extent, because you spend a lot of time at work. Depending on your working hours your whole social structure might change based on when you are expected to be wide awake at work.

Make sure you are ready to get the job, accept the right job for you, keep the job and understand your role and rights within the company. Do not be ashamed of your past and how much or how little you know. Rather be safe than sorry. Make sure you understand how to do the job safely. Do not play with your safety.

I wish you all the best in your career, and first in this, your first job.

Want more?

Please review this book to help me improve on my next books. More importantly, your reviews will help fellow new workers find the help they need to enter the work environment.

Please visit https://sites.google.com/view/goc-rsa/home for a free reference guide.

About the Author

Andreas holds a PhD in Chemistry and has applied the theory of constraints in manufacturing and supply chain management while being a Process Technologist, Production Manager and Plant Manager.

Andreas' work experience is in the managerial field (between thirty and 130 direct and indirect reports), technical field (product development, chemistry, spectroscopy, standards writing, statistics), industrial relations, OSH act, quality audits, training, lean, budgets and theory of constraints.

Andreas is a member of several societies:

Associate Member of the South African Chemical Institute (SACI)

Professional Provident Society

Plastics Institute of South Africa (PISA)

South African Council for Natural Scientific Professions

Theory of Constraints International Certification Organization

Institute of Directors – Southern Africa

What I believe

I believe that God created me to love him.

I believe that, before I met God, I was lost - in sin.

I believe that the only way to not be lost is to be with God.

I believe that nothing I can do can restore my relationship with God.

I believe Jesus came as God to die on the cross to make it possible for me to have a relationship with God.

I believe that because Jesus made the relationship between God and myself possible, I have eternal life.

I believe that I Jesus' sacrifice saved me.

I believe that I grow every day in the relationship with God - in the victory he has given me.

To learn more about what this can mean for you contact your local Christian Church.

www.ingramcontent.com/pod-product-compliance
Lightning Source LLC
Chambersburg PA
CBHW030444220526
45464CB00006B/2415